Teens and Sexting

Patricia D. Netzley

ReferencePoint Press®

San Diego, CA

© 2016 ReferencePoint Press, Inc.
Printed in the United States

For more information, contact:
ReferencePoint Press, Inc.
PO Box 27779
San Diego, CA 92198
www.ReferencePointPress.com

LIBRARY OF CONGRESS CATALOGING-IN-PUBLICATION DATA

Netzley, Patricia D.
  Teens and sexting / by Patricia D. Netzley.
    pages cm. -- (Teen choices)
  Includes bibliographical references and index.
  ISBN-13: 978-1-60152-916-9 (hardback)
  ISBN-10: 1-60152-916-3 (hardback)
  1. Sexting--Juvenile literature. 2. Teenagers--Sexual behavior--Juvenile literature. 3. Internet and teenagers--Juvenile literature. I. Title.
  HQ27.N47 2016
  306.70835--dc23
                                                            2014048805

Contents

Unforeseen Consequences

The word *sexting* originated as a reference to the act of using a cell phone to text, or send electronically, a sexually provocative or sexually explicit message or image. But social networking apps, instant messaging through websites like Facebook, and other advances in communication have made it possible to disseminate such messages and images in many different ways, using many different devices. Consequently, the word *sexting* now refers to sharing sexual content using electronic devices and cellular and online networks, although a cell or smart phone is still the most common means for teenagers to exchange sexts.

Regardless of the means of sexting, many teens see nothing wrong with the activity. Surveys suggest that 50 percent of those under the age of eighteen have engaged in some form of sexting and at least 20 percent have sent someone a sexually explicit photograph or video. (The legal definition of a sexually explicit photo is one that depicts someone engaged in a sexual act, posed in a sexually-explicit manner, or otherwise sexually excited.) Moreover, in speaking with researchers on the subject, many teens display a casual attitude toward sexting. As one high school girl told an interviewer with the Pew Internet & American Life Project, "Yeah, I've sent [sexts] to my boyfriend. Everybody does it."[1] A high school boy echoed this sentiment by saying, "I only do it with my girlfriend [because] we have already been sexually active with each other. It's not really a big deal."[2]

Legal Problems

But researchers have also found that a majority of teens do not realize this behavior can have serious consequences. For example, some teens experience legal problems as a result of their sexting. This is because under federal and many state laws the possession of a sexually explicit image of a minor is a crime, as is the sending of such an image to someone. In fact, even a person who receives an unrequested sexually explicit photo of a minor can be prosecuted for keeping it—and it does not matter whether the individual shown in the photo gave permission for his or her photograph to be taken.

Indeed, a teenager who takes a sexually explicit selfie and sexts it to someone else can be charged with three felony crimes: promoting, distributing, and possessing child pornography. Consequently, as psychologist James Wellborn reports, "[Students] don't understand the profound legal implications. They think they're just trading pictures. [The potential for criminal charges] puts a whole new developmental twist on this regular developmental process that teens go through."[3]

Such charges can come with the risk of lengthy prison sentences. In the state of Illinois, for example, anyone who videotapes or photographs a sexually excited nude or seminude person whom he or she should know is under the age of eighteen can be charged with a Class 1 felony. This charge comes with a mandatory fine of $2,000 to $100,000 and at least four years of prison. No exception is made for offenders who sent sexually explicit videos or photos of themselves.

In cases involving the widespread dissemination of such photos, the punishment can be even more severe. For example, thirty high school boys in Michigan are currently facing felony charges for sharing and collecting sexually explicit photos of

> "[Students] don't understand the profound legal implications [of sexting]. They think they're just trading pictures."[3]
>
> —Psychologist James Wellborn.

Once teens send sexually explicit photos of themselves over the Internet, they no longer have control over those images. If these pictures are further disseminated, they can be used to humiliate or bully their victims.

female classmates. Even though the girls provided the photos to the boys willingly, the boys could face prison sentences of as long as twenty years.

Sharing with Others

Sexting can also put teenagers at risk of embarrassment, because the recipients of sexts often see nothing wrong with showing other people what they received. For example, seventeen-year-old Matthew Younger of Maryland, who believes that sexting is "not a big deal," says: "If a boy meets a girl or has a girlfriend on summer break he comes back and shows all his boys the [naked] pictures he's been sent. No one gives it that much thought really."[4]

Some of those entrusted with sexts also think nothing of sharing sexually provocative and/or explicit photos online via websites such as Facebook. Depending on where the photos are posted they can remain online forever, causing difficulties for teenagers for years to come. In fact, there have been cases of people losing college scholarships or not getting certain jobs because sexually provocative or explicit photos of themselves were found online.

There have also been cases of teens being bullied because their sexted photos were shared with others. For example, in 2009 thirteen-year-old Hope Witsell was bullied at her middle school after a photo of her breasts that she had sexted to her boyfriend was discovered on his cellphone by a girl who disliked her. This girl then sexted the photo to students at several different schools in the area, who in turn shared it with others and began posting horrible things about Witsell online. As a result, Witsell committed suicide.

> "If a boy meets a girl or has a girlfriend on summer break he comes back and shows allhis boys the [naked] pictures he's been sent. No one gives it that much thought really."[4]
>
> —Seventeen-year-old Matthew Younger of Maryland.

Educating People

Given that sexting can lead to such serious problems, many people argue that teens need to be made more aware of the risks associated with the activity. For example, David De-Matteo, a professor of law and psychology at Drexel University in Philadelphia, Pennsylvania, says, "Young people need to be educated about the potential consequences of sexting—legal, social, and psychological. The education should come from many sources—the more young people hear the message, the more likely it will be to sink in—so they should be educated by their parents, schools, and perhaps even law enforcement."[5]

Along with other researchers DeMatteo surveyed undergraduates at Drexel University. They discovered that those who had been fully aware as minors of what harms might befall them if they sexted were far less likely to engage in the behavior than those who were unaware of the risks. Consequently, he suggests that being more informed about the risks of sexting might deter teens from sexting. Other experts, however, say that the risky nature of sexting is part of its attraction to teens, many of whom view the activity as an illicit thrill. In addition, many teens think that while others might face serious consequences for their actions, such things will never happen to them.

> "Young people need to be educated about the potential consequences of sexting— legal, social, and psychological."[5]
>
> —David DeMatteo, a professor of law and psychology at Drexel University, Philadelphia, Pennsylvania.

Donald Lowe, a Virginia sheriff who has investigated sexting cases, faced this while trying to make teenagers understand that they were at risk of criminal prosecution for engaging in sexting. He reports that while he was talking to them, "They're just sitting there thinking, *Wah, wah, wah.* . . . It's not sinking in. Remember at that age, you think you're invincible, and you're going to do whatever the hell you want to do? We just couldn't get them past that."[6] Many experts say that this obstacle will make it difficult to convince teens that sexting can be bad for them.

Chapter One

What Is the Point of Sexting?

While many teens willingly engage in sexting, their number is difficult to determine. In large part this is because many teens are reluctant to open up to adults about their sexual behaviors, including sexting. This makes it difficult for researchers to convince teens to participate in surveys on the subject, especially because minors are typically required to get written permission from their parents in order to do so. In addition, many researchers conduct their surveys by calling teens at home, where parents might be listening in. As David DeMatteo says, "It's not unreasonable to think that someone may be reluctant to admit to certain behaviors when talking to researchers on a phone."[7]

Nonetheless, most researchers believe that roughly 40 percent of teens have sent and/or received sexually provocative messages, 20 percent have sexted and/or received sexually provocative images, and 25 percent of teens have sexted and/or received nude and/or seminude images. Interviews with high schoolers appear to confirm that teens sext comments far more frequently than they sext photos. However, there appears to be a difference between the sexting behavior of younger teens as opposed to older ones. Eighteen-year-old William, one of several teens interviewed by the *New York Times* on the subject of sexting, reports: "Photo sexting is done more in middle school when you just get this technology [cell phones] and you're horny." In contrast, according to seventeen-year-old Farrah, "As you get older, kids use raunchy texts more. They're things kids wouldn't want to say in person."[8]

Another of the teenagers interviewed by the *Times*, eighteen-year-old Rachel, provides an example of a sexting incident that took place in middle school: "In eighth grade, four girls were having a sleepover and they took off their clothes, covered themselves with whipped cream and sent pictures to boys of themselves licking it off. People forwarded it because it was gossip and scandalous. In middle school, that's really appealing."[9] Other teens have spoken about how common it is for both middle school and high school girls to sext a boy a selfie of her bare breasts, and to a far lesser extent for boys to sext girls a photo of their genitals.

> "As you get older, kids use raunchy texts more. They're things kids wouldn't want to say in person."[8]
>
> —Seventeen-year-old Farrah, to a reporter for the New York Times.

Attention Seeking

Interviews and surveys have also suggested what motivates teens to sext. Among the most common is to attract the attention of others, as seventeen-year-old Taylor Weekes confirmed to a reporter with the UK's BBC: "Most girls of my generation do it for attention, to try and find love out of it, but it usually is the wrong way."[10]

This was apparently the case with several Illinois girls who sexted nude or seminude photos of themselves to members of their high school's basketball team in 2013. Those on the team who received the photos shared them with those who had not received them. When school officials found out about these activities they suspended those students who were involved in the sexting and pulled the team from the state playoffs. This led some of the other students at the school to complain that such punishment was unwarranted because the sexting did not hurt any of those who engaged in it.

This attitude is common among teens who sext. As Michael Ferjak of the Iowa Department of Justice says, "To them it's just

30 seconds of fun, 30 seconds of bad judgment without any consideration for what that leads to or could lead to."[11] This is certainly the case for the 40 percent of teens who have sexted as a joke. Often these jokes are simply intended to fluster someone, much like a prank from the days before cell phones when teens would slip into a photo booth to take pictures of naked body parts they could leave for others to find.

Many teens send selfies to friends because it is fun. But those who send sexually explicit selfies might be seeking attention or hoping to impress a boyfriend or girlfriend.

Sexting Acronyms

Although many teens do not worry about getting arrested because of their sexting, most do worry that their parents will check their phones, text messages, e-mails, or social media posts. Consequently, when writing racy remarks they might use acronyms to disguise the true meaning of their messages. Common sexting acronyms include IWS for "I want sex," GYPO for "Get your pants off," and TDTM for "Talk dirty to me." There are also acronyms to signal when parents are nearby. These include PIR for "Parents in room," CD9 or Code 9 for "Adult here," and 99 for "Parent has left."

Clinical psychologist Catherine Steiner-Adair interviewed teenagers about sexting while writing her book *The Big Disconnect: Protecting Childhood and Family Relationships in the Digital Age*. She reports that one boy told her his friends had pranked him by sexting crude messages to girls from his Facebook page, thereby making it look like he had sent the messages. She was surprised to discover that the boy was not upset by this—in fact, he found it funny—and that it did not cause any lasting problems in his relationship with the girls.

But sometimes what a sexter views as funny is interpreted by others as harmful, and this can lead to trouble. For example, three teenage boys in Virginia took cell phone videos in 2013 of themselves having consensual sex with several teenage girls, then they got drunk and sexted the videos to a social media site without the girls' consent. As a result, the boys were arrested and charged for unlawfully filming and distributing pornography. One of the teens later justified his actions by saying, "We had impaired judgment and we thought it was funny. I suppose you could call it a prank."[12] Experts say that it is not unusual for teens to sext impulsively while drunk or high.

Attracting Romance

Another common reason teens sext is out of the need to feel better about themselves in some way. For example, experts say that roughly 35 percent of teens sext in order to feel sexually desirable. Arlene Krieger, a certified sexologist practicing in Florida, equates sexting to other activities that once filled this need, saying: "Maybe forty years ago girls wanted to be cheerleaders. Nowadays, many girls engage in sexting to feel sexy, desired and popular."[13]

According to psychologist Elizabeth Englander, director of the Massachusetts Aggression Reduction Center at Bridgewater State University in Massachusetts, teenage girls also sext because they think it will get them a boyfriend. She explains that some girls fantasize that "if they sext, the popular people will see them as daring and self-confident, and they could get a boyfriend they wouldn't otherwise have gotten."[14] Indeed, 66 percent of teens who engage in sexting view it as a form of flirtation, whether with a potential partner or an existing one.

In addition, 52 percent of girls say that they have sexted a nude or seminude image to a boyfriend as a way to give him a present. In fact, the majority of teens who have created naked, semi-naked, or otherwise seductive photos of themselves send them privately to a boyfriend or girlfriend. Studies indicate that roughly 70 percent of such images are sent to a romantic partner. Most of those who send a sext to a boyfriend or girlfriend expect the recipient to keep the image or message private between the two of them.

As a result, experts say that sexting is increasingly being used as a way to show trust in a romantic partner. In writing about this trend, James Hamblin of the *Atlantic* says: "The fact

> "Maybe forty years ago girls wanted to be cheerleaders. Nowadays, many girls engage in sexting to feel sexy, desired and popular."[13]
>
> —*Arlene Krieger, a certified sexologist practicing in Florida.*

you're trusting the other person with that intimate moment, in all its permanence, is itself a primary virtue of sexting. 'Here. You could ruin me with this, but I trust you won't.' In the same way that an engagement ring is a symbol of sacrifice for another person, sexting can function as a symbol of commitment and trust, if subconsciously."[15]

> "The fact you're trusting the other person with that intimate moment, in all its permanence, is itself a primary virtue of sexting. 'Here. You could ruin me with this, but I trust you won't.'"[15]
>
> —James Hamblin of the Atlantic.

Interviews with teenagers indicate that sexting is also considered an intimate form of conversation. Eighteen-year-old Saif of Brooklyn, New York, told the *Times* interviewers, "It's a way to express your feelings. If a guy and a girl are in love, instead of saying it face to face, they can say it through technology."[16]

Initiating a Relationship

But sometimes intimate sexting occurs between a boy and a girl before they have even developed a relationship. A study of Texas teens who answered an anonymous survey found that one in four teens sent a sexually provocative message to someone with whom they were interested in establishing a relationship. Usually this is a classmate, but some studies have found that roughly 15 percent of teens who have sexted nude and/or seminude images of themselves have sent them to people they have interacted with only online.

In either case, according to a 2012 study of teen sexting behaviors in the UK, it is more common for a girl than a boy to sext a photo for the purposes of initiating a relationship, although the sexting might be done because of a boy's request. In writing about the study results Andy Phippen, a professor of social responsibility in information technology, explains that "boys would request pictures of girls and girls *may* send pictures as a result of these invitations. It was considered highly unusual for a girl to request a picture of a boy. . . . [But while] girls were far more likely to be the recipient of a request many we spoke to . . . were clear that for anyone it was their choice, and responsibility, to respond to a request. Just because a boy asked for a picture it did not mean they had to respond."[17] Phippen also reports that girls typically felt flattered and attractive for being asked to sext a photo, even when they were aware that the boy who asked might be asking other girls as well.

However, there are also cases where girls send photos to a boy without first being asked to do so. This was the case with fourteen-year-old Michael Harmon, who was taken aback when a female classmate sent him a photo of her naked breasts. He had never received such an image before, but he did not find it objectionable. He says, "I was like, wow. I was shocked, but

Roughly two-thirds of teens view sexting as a form of flirtation. They imagine the provocative text or images will make them seem confident and eager to spark or maintain a romance with the intended recipient.

I was kind of happy, too. I bragged about that first one to my friends, but I didn't show them the photo. It wasn't anybody's business. After a few days, I deleted it."[18]

Hooking Up

When a boy sexts a photo of himself to a girl, it is often to signal that he is interested in her sexually. One teenage girl told researchers from the Pew Research Center in 2009, "If a guy wants to hookup with you, he'll send a picture of his private parts or a naked picture of him[self]. It happens about 10 times a month."[19]

Hookups are typically defined as sexual encounters undertaken with no promise that they will lead to any sort of meaningful relationship between the participants. Such encounters do not have to involve intercourse; any kind of sexual activity, including kissing and/or fondling, qualifies. According to experts in sexual behavior, hookups are a trend among teens, many of whom have no interest in anything deeper than a sexual encounter, and sexting is a common way to initiate this activity. In fact, psychologist Jeff Temple of the University of Texas Medical Branch at Galveston, head of the Texas study on teenage sexting, reports that in his own study on teen sexting "sexting preceded sexual behavior in many cases. The theory behind that is sexting may act as a gateway or prelude to sexual behaviors or increases the acceptance of going to the next level."[20]

Temple and an associate who worked on the study, Hye Jeong Choi, also found that teens were more likely to be sexually active when they were juniors in high school if they had sexted at least one nude picture of themselves during the previous year. Other researchers have found that teens who have been sexually active are more likely to sext than those who have never had sex. In addition, teens who are gay, lesbian, or bisexual are more likely to be involved in sexting than students who are heterosexual.

However, Choi notes that there is a difference in regard to sexuality between those who receive sexts and those who

Celebgate

In September 2014 several celebrities learned that private photos on a personal smartphone are not necessarily safe from other people's eyes. Copies of such photos are also typically stored in a secure account on the Internet. Somehow hackers managed to access the celebrities' accounts (most likely by guessing their passwords) and share the photos online. Over one hundred celebrity accounts were hacked, and experts estimate that they were shared online over a billion times. Many of the photos showed a celebrity nude or seminude and/or in a sexually suggestive pose.

In commenting on this incident, the website nobullying.com says that the fact that the photos are all over the Internet "saddens every woman who can sense the amount of predators and perverts out there with no respect for the meaning of privacy." The website also criticizes people for saying horrible things about the actresses' decision to take nude or sexually suggestive photos of themselves. The site says: "There is no proof any of the people involved were sexting or sending those photos to others. For all we know, they were taking those photos of themselves to examine their bodies or in celebration of their form. And what honestly matters, is that they are private photos meant for private viewing."

Nobullying.com, "What Really Happened in Celebgate?," September 2014. http://nobullying.com.

send them. He explains, "Being a passive recipient of or asking for a sext does not likely require the same level of comfort with one's sexuality. Sending a nude photo may communicate to the recipient a level of openness to sexual activity, promote a belief that sex is expected, and serve to increase sexual advances, all of which may increase the chance of future sexual behavior."[21]

But other researchers have found that sexting can be used as a way to experiment with sexual behavior without having to deal with possible consequences. For example, Sameer Hinduja, an expert in cyberbullying who has surveyed teens on sexting behavior, says: "In our culture, sexting can be construed as a way for adolescents to explore their sexuality without actually participating in the act of sex. Indeed, several teens have told us that they engage in sexting because 'it is safer than having sex.' They don't have to worry about getting pregnant or contracting a disease."[22]

My Life, My Body

Another aspect of teenage sexuality that encourages sexting is how young people view their own bodies. Many of them believe that people should have the right to do whatever they want with their own bodies, including sharing photos of it. Consequently Susan Lipkins, a Port Washington, New York, psychologist who has studied adolescent behavior, says sexting may be a symptom of a sexual revolution, with the sharing of sexual material becoming commonplace. She says, "Sexting is just the tip of the iceberg. It's a reflection of casual sex, [changes in] the way [teens] look at their bodies, the way they look at privacy, ownership, physical and personal space."[23]

As an example of how teens express these attitudes, girls being interviewed as part of an investigation into a 2014 sexting case in Virginia told police that they saw nothing wrong with their sending nude or seminude photos of themselves to boys. One of them said, "This is my life and my body and I can do whatever I want with it."[24] Another insisted, "I don't see any problem with it. I'm proud of my body."[25] Moreover, according to Donald Lowe, who headed the investigation, many of the girls were far more upset with having to be interviewed by police than they were with the boys who had shared their photos via Instagram without consent.

Collecting Images

The Virginia Instagram case involved over one hundred teens in six counties who shared over one thousand sexted photographs and videos, which makes it one of the largest known teen sexting rings. (In law enforcement circles, a group of peo-

18

ple who join together in the commission of a crime is known as a ring.) But experts suspect there are more such rings waiting to be discovered. This is because some boys collect and share sexted images the way younger boys collect and share Pokémon or other game cards. As one high school boy told a researcher with the Pew Internet & American Life Project, "Sometimes people trade pictures like 'hey you send me a pic I'll send you one.'"[26]

In some cases, the girls providing the images know that they are being collected and shared. Such was the case with a Michigan sexting ring that came to the attention of authorities in mid-September 2014. The participants were thirty high school boys and one middle school boy who decided to start collecting nude photos of female classmates. Attorney Shannon Smith, who is representing two of the boys against charges related to creating, soliciting, distributing, and/or possessing child pornography, says of the boys' activities, "They were asking girls to text them nude photos. The girls were cooperating and then the boys were trading the pictures — giving them to other people. There were a lot of girls that were sending photos, and it just got out of control."[27]

> "Sexting is just the tip of the iceberg. It's a reflection of casual sex, [changes in] the way [teens] look at their bodies, the way they look at privacy, ownership, physical and personal space."[23]
>
> —New York psychologist Susan Lipkins.

It is more common, however, for the girls who provide photos of themselves not to know they are intended to be shared. Studies have shown that three-fourths of girls who sext a nude or seminude photo of themselves to a boy do not give their consent for it to be shared with anyone else. Nonetheless, 17 percent of teens who receive a sexted nude or seminude photo, even one from a romantic partner, do show it to someone else. In fact, 55 percent of those who share the image show it to more than one other person.

Sexted messages, however, appear to be less likely to be shared. In his interview with a reporter from the *New York Times*, eighteen-year-old William explains, "If a girl sent me a picture of her boobs, well, obviously I'd like to show it to some friends. But I wouldn't show them a raunchy text from her because that would be awkward. Sexually charged language is more intimate, more private."[28]

Intending to Hurt

But when a relationship goes bad, intimate messages and images can be shared out of anger and a desire to hurt an ex-partner. The means of exacting revenge might be to forward the image to all of the ex's friends, but more typically it is to share the image online. As one older high school boy told a Pew researcher: "This girl sent pictures to her boyfriend. Then they broke up and he sent them to his friend, who sent them to like everyone in my school."[29] Another teen, nineteen-year-old Daniel, told a reporter with the BBC that the day after a girl sexted him a picture of herself, the two argued over something else, and "I got so angry, I was sending that picture everywhere. It was mean. I felt bad after. To this day she hates me, but that's not the point. I shouldn't have done it in the first place."[30]

Alternatively, a girlfriend might sext a boyfriend or ex-boyfriend a photo of herself engaging in sexual behavior with another person as a way to make him jealous. There have also been cases of teenage girls posting sexted photos online of a boyfriend's ex-girlfriend after finding them on his cell phone. Similarly, two girls in Ohio who were both interested in the same boy shared sexted images of each other online as a way to attack one another. But in this case the activity soon escalated to include at least thirty other participants. This was because the two girls who started the sexting attacks belonged to two rival groups, and members of both groups started posting images of each other as well. The resulting series of retaliations went on for two years, until police arrested one of the initial posters in October 2014.

After a breakup, it is not uncommon for jealous or vengeful boyfriends or girlfriends to repost sexts from their partners to punish or embarrass them. Once those images are disseminated, anyone can use them to bully the victim or cause further humiliation.

A Normal Activity

Such cases get a lot of media attention. However, some researchers say that the odds that sexually explicit or provocative sexts will be shared publicly is relatively small. According to sexting researcher Heidi Strohmaier of Drexel University: "Although youth sexting is quite common, it tends to occur among consenting romantic partners and rarely results in the catastrophic consequences often portrayed in the media."[31]

Elizabeth Englander agrees that the risk is less than media reports suggest. In fact, she says that her own research indicates that more than three-fourths of teens who sext do not believe that their photos went to anyone but the intended recipient. She acknowledges that those who say their photos have gone to no one else could be mistaken, but she is inclined to believe that they would know if their sexts were being passed around to a degree that would cause trauma.

In any case, Englander has no problems with sexting as long as the sexter is not coerced into participating in the activity. This is because she views it as a normal part of adolescent sexual development, akin to forms of sexual flirtation and exploration that have existed for generations. And indeed, the motivations for sexting—which include wanting to engage in flirting or intimate conversation, to show trust in a partner, to feel sexy, and to give a gift to a boyfriend or girlfriend—have existed long before the invention of cell phones.

Chapter Two

Outside Influences

Teens have many personal reasons for wanting to sext, but the decision to engage in sexting can also be influenced by peers, by the media, by society at large, and by the nature of the developing teenage brain. This pressure to sext can be strong or mild, but experts say that in either case teens who feel pushed into sexting typically do not like the experience. In fact, according to Elizabeth Englander, 68 percent of teens who felt pressured into sexting said afterward that their sexting had been harmful.

Boyfriend Pressures

Englander's studies indicate that two-thirds of teens have been pressured into sexting something they did not really want to sext. Other studies suggest that three times more girls than boys are pressured into sexting. In the case of girls who are pressured, most often the coercion takes place as part of a boyfriend-girlfriend relationship that is either longstanding or just beginning. Such was the case with twelve-year-old Michaela Snyder of Minnesota. She had dated her boyfriend for only a month when he insisted she sext him nude photos of herself. "He wanted pictures from me. He wanted to see my body," she explains. "He just texted one day and said, 'You should do it.' I said no. He said, 'If you love me, you'll do it, if not, I'll leave you.'"[32]

Michaela asked her friends what she should do, and they advised her to go ahead and sext her boyfriend the photos he wanted. After all, they told her, sexting is perfectly normal.

Consequently, she sexted him a picture of herself in her underwear. "He then started asking for more, more naked pictures. I never sent those. I was never going to send that,"[33] Michaela says.

After Michaela's mother found the sext on her cell phone and told her father—a police sergeant who investigates juvenile sex crimes—about it, Michaela was in trouble. Her parents went to the boy's parents to tell them what he had done and ensure he was punished. Soon her classmates found out about this and she was hassled at school. In 2014, two years after the sexting incident, she told a reporter that it took her two years to stop feeling bad about what she now calls her "stupid choices."[34] She also told him that she was coming forward with her story in hope of preventing others from making the same mistakes.

> "He wanted pictures from me. He wanted to see my body. . . . He said, 'If you love me, you'll do it, if not, I'll leave you.'"[32]
>
> —*Twelve-year-old Michaela Snyder of Minnesota speaking of her boyfriend.*

Boys as Victims

In reporting on coerced sexting among teens, the media tends to focus on stories like Michaela's that feature the boy as the aggressor and the girl as the victim. But boys can be victimized by coerced sexting as well. Psychologist Jill Murray reports: "I'm finding this very much in high schools and it's a very disturbing trend where girls choose a boy who is sexually naïve and she asks for pictures of him. He's sort of flattered and he feels like a big guy and then she sends them around."[35] Murray and other experts say that a boy can be just as devastated as a girl over such a betrayal. Moreover, when sexted photos are shared among classmates, both boys and girls can be just as brutally teased about their physical appearance.

Experts also say that when boys pressure one another to sext or to get girls to sext they are promoting an attitude that is bad for their own emotional development—specifically, the idea that boys are predators and girls are prey. Clinical psychologist Catherine Steiner-Adair suggests that when boys are pushed into adopting this view, it can damage their ability to form healthy relationships as adults. She says, "It's such a bad

Most media stories involving sexting portray girls as the victims, but boys can also fall prey to the abuse. Some boys may sext messages or photos to feel manlier, only to be embarrassed when these words and images are spread beyond their control.

Communication Struggles

Experts say that when people grow up communicating with peers primarily via text messages, they can fail to learn how to interact successfully with others in person. This is because they have not developed the ability to read body language and facial expressions. In addition, according to clinical psychologist Catherine Steiner-Adair, a texting exchange can be so fast-paced that it "deletes the pause" between thinking something and saying something. Consequently texting is the "worst possible training ground" for how to develop a meaningful relationship. Similarly, Dan Slater, another expert in the effect of texting on relationships, says that while texting is a valid form of exchanging messages, it does not provide opportunities to learn how to deal with "messy relationship stuff." And as he points out, "That's the stuff that helps people grow up."

Quoted in Abigail Pesta, "Boys Also Harmed by Teen 'Hook-Up' Culture, Experts Say," NBC News, August 14, 2013. www.nbcnews.com.

part of our culture to think that boys aren't also harmed. We are neglecting the emotional lives of boys."[36]

Researchers with the Institute of Education, King's College London, London School of Economics and Open University agree with this position. In writing about their own 2012 study of sexting behavior among teens they say:

> We need gender sensitive support that does not treat sexting as the fault of girls, and also we cannot simply demonize boys. Many existing resources are based on sexual stereotypes and worst case scenarios, are moralising and implicitly place the burden of blame on girls for sending a photo, thereby reproducing the problematic message that girls are to protect their innocent virginal body from the predatory over-sexed male. This in itself is a form of victimization [of both boys and girls], which can be harmful.[37]

The London researchers also note that modern society has created a global consumer culture that is both sexist and sexualized. In a sexist culture, women are often objectified, as is evident when men swap pictures of women as though they were trading cards. In a sexualized culture, many of the culture's attributes, such as fashions and movies, have some sexual association. Many experts say that American culture is so extreme in this regard that it can be considered hypersexualized. Within this environment, people tend to spend a great deal of time thinking about and talking about sex.

Cultural Influences

Among teens this preoccupation with sex is apparent even at school. As an example, *Vanity Fair* magazine reporter Nancy Jo Sales reports that a teenager attending a New York public school told her: "My little cousin, she's 13, and she posts such inappropriate pictures on Instagram, and boys post sexual comments, and she's like, 'Thank you.' It's child pornography, and everyone's looking at it on their iPhones in the cafeteria."[38]

Experts say that being steeped in a hypersexualized culture makes girls more likely to engage in self-sexualization. Signs of self-sexualization include buying certain products and clothes out of a desire to look sexy, trying to look and behave like celebrities who are known for their sexiness, and expressing attitudes that support the sexualization of women. Learning to make choices in regard to sexual behavior is a normal part of sexual development. But experts also note that self-sexualization promotes the idea that how a woman's body looks is more important than her mind, thereby turning her into little more than a visual object. This means that teenage girls are contributing to their own objectification, the treating of a person as a thing.

However, sexualization makes it difficult to determine whether any particular decision is truly made with free will. Abigail M.

Judge, a clinical psychologist in Massachusetts who is also an expert on the psychology of sexting, explains:

> The practice of youth-produced sexual images suggests the ways in which healthy sexual exploration and the processes of sexualization may blur for girls. . . . The question of self-motivated sexual action around youth-produced sexual images is an important, if thorny, matter: to what extent do youth freely participate in these behaviors, or do so because they feel that, based on interpersonal and social norms, it is expected?[39]

Some experts who work with teens say that television is particularly influential in regard to encouraging girls to self-sexualize. For example, Kim Goldman, the director of a counseling service for teens in Santa Clarita, California, says, "Girls talk about feeling like they have to be like what they see on TV. They talk about body-image issues and not having any role models. They all want to be like the Kardashians. Kendall Jenner posts bikini shots when she's 16 and gets 10,000 likes, and girls see that's what you do to get attention."[40]

Competing Pressures

Other experts point out that among certain groups of girls, not participating in such behavior will lead to rejection by the group. This can involve not only exclusion but name-calling. For example, teenage girls who refuse to sext are often called "prude" or "stuck up."

But girls who do engage in such behavior might be called names as well—usually "whore" or "slut." For some girls, the fear of attracting such labels keeps them from sexting; for others, the fear of being labeled a prude encourages them to sext. However, according to a University of Michigan (U-M) study reported in the *Journal of Children and Media* in 2014, boys are not subjected to the same treatment. Whether they sext or not, most face no criticism.

U-M researchers Julia R. Lippman and Scott W. Campbell also found that boys are often the ones promoting the labeling of girls who sext. In responding to the researchers' open-ended questionnaires, a fourteen-year-old boy said, "I have received some pics that include nudity. Girls will send them sometimes, not often. I don't know why they think it's a good idea but I'm not going to stop it . . . I like classy girls so I don't like them as much anymore it makes them look slutty." In contrast, teenage girls told of boys pressuring them into sexting. One said, "My boyfriend or someone I really liked asked for them. And I felt like if I didn't do it, they wouldn't continue to talk to me." Another reported, "Guys ask for them and if we don't send them they will think we aren't outgoing and get mad."[41]

Reality television star Kendall Jenner is known for propelling her modeling career by posting pictures of herself on Instagram. Some critics believe teens who follow celebrity trends feel less fear in posing for and posting pictures on social media sites.

The Sexting Culture

Smith blames boys for creating a sexting culture, one that both pushes girls into sexting and then punishes them for doing so. But it is difficult for teens of both genders to resist sexting given the way the activity is supported by modern technology. As one teenage boy says: "Nowadays you can do it so easy. There are so many apps . . . that just, like, hand you the girls. They don't even know that's what they're doing, but really they're just giving teenagers ways to have sex."[42]

Among the most popular such applications is Snapchat, released to the public in 2011. According to Snapchat, 350 million photos, which it calls Snaps, are transmitted every day via its network. The photo-messaging app's popularity stems from the fact that the sender of a Snap can limit the amount of time the recipient can view it to just a few seconds. Once the time has expired the Snap is no longer viewable on the recipient's device, and it is deleted from the Snapchat server. The image also disappears during the viewing period if the recipient stops touching the screen for even a moment, which makes taking a screenshot of the image difficult.

But security experts warn that while the Snap can no longer be viewed on the recipient's device, it is still on the device and merely hidden. This means that someone who knows how to access the image can sext it, just as someone who manages to take a screenshot of the image can sext it. Nonetheless, because of Snap's apparent impermanence, Jack, a college student who uses Snapchat, says that when the app was released it revolutionized sexting. He reports that after that release the number of sexts he received increased dramatically. He also began sending more sexts himself. He says, "People feel much better about themselves with the use of Snapchat. Sending a nude pic and knowing people won't be able to see it again unless they snapshot it thrills the hell out of people. . . . I've sent a couple of pics over Snapchat that I may regret, but knowing that the person won't be able to see it again is reassuring."[43]

Another photo-sharing app that makes sexting easier is Instagram, which allows people to post photos for followers who can add comments to them. In late 2013 the company added a private messaging service, Instagram Direct, that allows people to sext one-on-one. However, as with Snapchat, users can take screenshots of these private messages to save and perhaps forward.

Two other apps that are popular for sexting are Kik and Vine. Kik is an instant messaging app similar to texting. However, it also provides the ability to share photos and files and to chat in groups. Vine is a video-sharing app that allows users to record videos of a few seconds and then share them with users of Twitter and Facebook. All Vine accounts are public by default,

Free Speech

In the United States freedom of speech is protected by the First Amendment of the Constitution. This means that people can say whatever they want—with some exceptions. The US Supreme Court has recognized that certain types of speech are excluded from First Amendment protections, and it allows governments to enact reasonable restrictions on speech as well. Consequently, the state of Texas felt it was on sound legal ground when in 2005 it enacted a statute making sexually explicit online communications between an adult and minor illegal. This law was then used to prosecute adults who were sexting raunchy messages to teens. One such case involved a thirty-year-old middle school teacher, Sean Williams, who was exchanging sexts with a thirteen-year-old female student. One of these communications included a photo of the girl's bare breasts. Nonetheless, in February 2014 prosecutors felt they had to drop the charges against Williams. This decision was based on an October 2013 Texas appeals court ruling in another case involving a teacher sending sexually graphic messages to a student. In that case the court found that the 2005 ban on such communications violated the First Amendment by not being specific enough as to what constituted sexually explicit speech as opposed to sexually indecent speech. This appeals court decision and prosecutors' response to it has outraged many Texas parents, who had applauded the law for protecting children against sexual predators.

although users can set up a protected account, and people who have downloaded the Vine app can view other Vine users' public videos, even sexually explicit ones.

Adult Predators

Sexting apps not only make it easy for teens to share sexts with one another, they make it easier for adults to sext minors—and many of these adults are sexual predators skilled at coercing teens into taking and sharing sexually explicit photos and videos of themselves. In fact, according to cybersafety expert Susan McLean, the author of *Sexts, Texts & Selfies*, "Kik is the number one app for sex predators worldwide. Within Kik itself there are probably 20 adult content apps that you can connect into and predators love it because they know there are so many kids on there unsupervised and unmonitored."[44]

The coercion by a sexual predator typically takes place gradually as part of a process known as grooming. Initial conversations in this process are usually innocent, as the predator—most often a male—tries to create a rapport with the victim. To this end the predator will often pretend to be the same age as the victim or not mention age at all and will talk about things that young people are interested in, such as popular celebrities or trends. He will also typically sympathize with the victim's problems, giving the victim the feeling that he is the only person who truly understands how the young person feels.

Once the predator senses that the victim has developed some measure of trust in him, he will begin to initiate sexually charged conversations, testing to see whether the victim can be encouraged to talk about such things. Once this willingness is evident, the predator might then send the victim pornography before beginning to urge the victim to sext nude selfies.

The Teenage Brain

Experts say that teens are more susceptible to this kind of pressure because their brains are not fully developed. Specifically, the prefrontal cortex—the area of the brain responsible for problem solving, decision making, and impulse control—does not reach full maturity until a person is in his or her early to mid-twenties. Consequently, experts say that young people are much more likely than mature adults to sext impulsively.

Judge says that this lack of restraint also affects the way young people think about, talk about, and absorb information about sexting. She explains:

> Sexting, consistent with neurobiological development, may be viewed as an emotionally driven behavior that is often impulsive and without a clear anticipation or understanding of the potential adverse consequences. An adolescent who speaks rationally about sexting when calm may nonetheless engage in the behavior (including in an aggravated manner) when emotionally aroused. Real-world decision making typically occurs under conditions of "hot cognition," or high emotional arousal. . . . [There is also typically a] wider distribution of sexual images . . . following a breakup, when emotional reactivity may trump careful reasoning.[45]

Risk Taking

The impulsivity of young people also leads them to be more likely to take risks, and their brain immaturity makes them less able to judge whether a particular activity is low-risk or high-risk. Experts say that in terms of learning, an inability to judge risks is a positive attribute because it makes young people more willing to try new things and explore new environments. But according to a 2012 study by researchers with New York University, it also makes teens more comfortable with uncertainty, particularly in regard to not knowing what the risks are. Consequently, teens not only misestimate risks but also tend to ignore details about specific risks. This means that many do not take risk statistics into account when deciding whether to do something. Studies have also shown that when deciding to engage in an activity, teens focus on its possible rewards, whereas adults focus on its potential consequences.

The Psychologically Unprepared

This difference in focus, experts say, along with teens' impulsivity, sexual immaturity, and susceptibility to cultural influences, all make young people more likely than adults to sext. (Although adults sext one another as well, and some—such as former congressman Anthony Weiner, who resigned office in 2011 after scandals related to his sexting—have gotten into trouble for their actions.) But as Judge points out, the key factor in sexting behavior is technology. She explains: "It is not that such developmental questions around sexuality, identity,

In 2011 married congressman Anthony Weiner of New York admitted that he used Twitter, Facebook, and e-mail to send sexually explicit photos of himself to women followers. The scandal caused him to resign from office that year.

and intimacy make technology inherently dangerous for teens; instead, the problem is that electronic devices may, in effect, usurp behavioral choices before an individual may be psychologically prepared."[46]

To illustrate this point, she quotes a high school senior who shows "retrospective clarity" and "the hindsight of psychological growth" in regard to her earlier sexting. According to Judge, the girl responded to a Pew survey: "When I was about 14–15 years old, I received/sent these types of pictures. Boys usually asked for them. . . . My boyfriend, or someone I really liked asked for them. And I felt like if I didn't do it they wouldn't continue to talk to me. At the time, I thought it was no big deal. But now looking back it was definitely inappropriate and over the line."[47]

> "The problem is that electronic devices may, in effect, usurp behavioral choices before an individual may be psychologically prepared."[46]
>
> —Massachusetts psychologist Abigail Judge.

Technology as a Cause

Sociologist Scarlett Brown agrees that it is common for people to view sexting differently as teens than they do as adults. She says: "I am part of the generation that first grew up with these forms of technology. I . . . have fond memories of how relationships were enacted in an online space. At the time, much like the teenagers in these studies, it did not occur to us that this behaviour might be risky or illegal. More importantly however, there was no sense that it was the technology itself that was causing this risk."[48]

Indeed, without access to mobile devices, teens would have a hard time sexting, particularly since a Pew Research survey released in March 2013 reveals that 71 percent of teens with a home computer (desktop or laptop) say that they share it with other family members. In contrast, mobile devices allow most teens enough privacy to conceal from adults the content of the messages and images they transmit.

The 2013 Pew survey found that 78 percent of teens have a cell phone, and 47 percent of those phones are smartphones. (This means that 37 percent of all teens have smartphones.) In addition, 23 percent of teens have a tablet computer. Approximately 74 percent of teens aged twelve to seventeen access the Internet on mobile devices, including cell phones and tablets, at least occasionally, and about 55 percent of older teenage girls access the Internet primarily from a smartphone.

> "I am part of the generation that first grew up with these forms of technology. . . . It did not occur to us that this behaviour might be risky or illegal."[48]
>
> —*Sociologist Scarlett Brown.*

Pew also reports that these numbers represent significant increases from 2011, and the use of mobile devices among teens continues to grow. Therefore it is understandable that teen sexting has increased during the same period. Moreover, because mobile devices make it possible for people to send messages from anywhere at any time, having such a device makes it more likely that a teen will sext impulsively—and as experts have noted, sexting that is done impulsively is often the kind that causes regrets.

Chapter Three

The Consequences of Sexting

Many teens report having experienced no negative consequences from sexting. Their sexts have gone to the intended recipients, no one has shared their messages or images without permission, and if their school is a place where kids commonly trade sexy photos, then it has been a harmless activity. Consequently, they believe that the media is exaggerating the dangers of sexting. In fact, this is a common view among teens who sext. A 2012 joint study by the University of South Carolina and the Chinese University of Hong Kong found that the majority of American teenagers who sext believe that while the activity might be harmful to other people, it is not and will not be harmful to them.

Some researchers partially support this view by saying that the odds of something bad happening to any one particular teen as a result of his or her sexting is slim. Elizabeth Englander, for example, says: "Research suggests that most photos don't end up in disasters, either socially (being passed around, teased, bullied) or criminally (being prosecuted). Such outcomes are possible, but they aren't highly probable."[49]

However, those teens who have suffered social, psychological, and/or legal problems as a result of their sexting often express the wish that they had not engaged in the activity and do not believe it was worth the outcome. An example of a teen who regrets sexting is fifteen-year-old Katherine Brochu of Montreal, Canada. When she was thirteen she sent nude photos of herself to a few boys who had asked for them. She explains the reason she did so: "I thought they would like me for my body and that they would appreciate me for that. That I would be loved by some guys because of how I looked." Instead, the boys shared the photo with nearly all of the boys in Brochu's high school. Her reputation suffered to a degree she never thought possible, and she lost her friends. When one of those friends told her parents what Brochu had done, Brochu also had to face her parents' disappointment in her. Consequently, she tells other teenage girls to think twice about taking and sexting sexy photos of themselves, saying, "It could be the worst mistake of your life."[50]

> ### "It could be the worst mistake of your life."[50]
>
> —Fifteen-year-old Katherine Brochu, who was harassed after sexting a nude selfie.

Can't Take It Back

Another sexter who deeply regrets her actions is Margarite of Lacey, Washington, who at the age of fourteen in late 2009 sexted a fellow eighth grade student, Isaiah, a nude photo of herself that subsequently went viral. Hundreds and perhaps thousands of teens in her area viewed the photo. This occurred because Isaiah had forwarded Margarite's sext to a classmate she was feuding with—although he later said that he did not realize this girl hated Margarite. That girl and a thirteen-year-old friend forwarded the picture to others after attaching a text message to it: "If you think this girl is a whore, then text this to all your friends."[51]

A year after the incident, Margarite was still being called vicious names by other teens in her area, and at least one teen who wanted to be Margarite's friend was called names, too. Therefore, when asked whether she has a message for other teens thinking of sexting, Margarite says: "If they are about to send a picture and they have a feeling, like, they're not sure they should, then don't do it at all. I mean, what are you thinking? It's freaking stupid!"[52]

Isaiah and the thirteen-year-old have also expressed regret for their actions. (The other girl appears to be without remorse.) All three of the teens responsible for forwarding the images to others were originally charged with disseminating child pornography, but this was later reduced to a misdemeanor charge of harassment. The three were ordered to do community service.

As part of this program, the teens made presentations to other teens. The thirteen-year-old told her audience: "I am a 13 year old teen that made a bad choice and got my life almost totaled forever. I regret what I did more than anything but I can't take it back."[53] Isaiah told them: "Not only does [sexting] hurt the people that are involved in the pictures you send, it can hurt your family and friends around you, the way they see you, the way you see yourself. The ways they feel about you. Them crying because of your mistakes."[54]

Making Life Unbearable

Prosecutors involved with Margarite's case decided not to charge her with any crime because they felt that she had already suffered enough from what had happened. Moreover, it

Sexting Altercations

Sexting nude photos can sometimes lead to violence. This is what happened in Fargo, North Dakota, in 2013 after a fifteen-year-old boy discovered that his thirteen-year-old sister had received photos of another fifteen-year-old boy's genitals via Snapchat. (Some teens refer to such photos as junkshot selfies.) Angered by the discovery, the brother sent a Snapchat message to the boy demanding that he show up at a local convenience store at a certain time to discuss the matter. During this meeting, the boy who sent the photos insisted that they were part of a consensual exchange of nude photos with the girl—which the girl denied. A fistfight ensued between the two boys. When the police arrived, the brother was the one bloodied from a cut on the face.

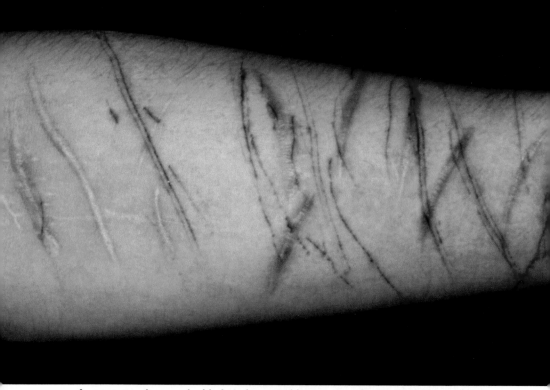

A young man has used a blade to lacerate his own arm. Such self-inflicted harm is a possible consequence of bottling up the shame and humiliation of having sext messages or images forever floating around on the Internet.

has proved impossible to remove all traces of her photo from the Internet, where some of those who received the forwarded image had posted it. Consequently, her father says, "She will have to live with this for the rest of her life."[55]

Experts in teen psychology, such as Raychelle Cassada Lohmann, say that repercussions of having one's nude or semi-nude selfie shared with others without permission can make life almost unbearable for teens. Many victims believe there is no way to make things better. Lohmann reports: "Oftentimes they don't reach out for help because of embarrassment and disappointment, fear of making it worse, or fear of getting into trouble. To many teens they may feel like they're caught in a trap with no way out."[56]

This feeling can cause teens to self-harm. Psychologist Jill Murray reports that two of the girls under her care have attempted suicide, and several others have had to switch schools because of sexting-related problems. She also reports that the most serious cases involve mass forwarding. She explains:

> For girls who send the sexts I think that there is a disillusionment and a sense of betrayal when it's posted everywhere. When it gets forwarded to multiple boys at multiple schools and also other girls . . . a girl starts getting called names and her reputation is ruined. . . . Of course, all of that leads to depression and regret. These girls may act real tough and say this doesn't matter but a lot of them do wind up doing some sort of self harm . . . cutting, bulimia, burning themselves, pulling out eyelashes or pubic hair, or some other sort of self-injurious behavior like alcohol and drug use."[57]

As with Murray's patients, most of those who suffer these effects are girls. Studies show that girls are subjected to harassment as a result of sharing nude or seminude selfies far more often than boys. Boys typically suffer less ridicule (or none at all) as a result of people seeing images of them naked or nearly so. Even so, the betrayal of having their photos shared without their consent can leave boys emotionally scarred. Seventeen-year-old James has experienced this firsthand. He has blogged about what he went through after someone took a screen shot of a video message he had sexted to a previous girlfriend and then posted the shot online. He reports, "They called me a pervert and lots of people I knew saw it—it was clearly me pictured. I was completely devastated and, to be honest, almost suicidal. I got the picture taken down eventually, but by that stage people had 'unfriended' me and the damage was done."[58]

> **"They called me a pervert and lots of people I knew saw it. . . . I was completely devastated and . . . almost suicidal."[58]**
>
> —Seventeen-year-old James, after someone took a screenshot of a video message he had sexted to a previous girlfriend and posted it online.

Driven to Suicide

The media has reported on a few cases of suicide tied to sexting-related harassment. One of the most prominent was that of eighteen-year-old Jessica Logan, an Ohio high school student. Logan's privacy was violated in 2008 while she was in Florida with friends during spring break. Unbeknownst to her, one of these friends took her phone, looked through its photos, found a nude selfie of Logan, and sexted it from Logan's cell phone to several other girls and to Logan's boyfriend. When Logan returned to school after the break, she could not understand why her classmates were pointing and laughing at her as she walked down the hallways and refusing to sit with her at lunch. Then a friend told her that her photo was on many of her classmates' cell phones, and those who had the photo were sending or showing it to others. Distraught, she and her parents complained to school officials about what was happening, but little was done and the harassment escalated. Logan's mother says:

> Jessica started receiving cell messages from strangers writing filthy names. I called two of [the] girls' parents, but they refused to do anything to help. Her high school peers were vicious. They called her every horrific name to degrade a human being as well as made fun of everything about her from her small stature to the texture of her hair. They dubbed her the "porn queen" and she became "that girl." Some told her no one cared about her and to go kill herself.[59]

These attacks did not stop even after Logan graduated, and shortly thereafter she hanged herself.

School Actions

Because of cases like Logan's many schools have taken a strong stance against sexting. This means that when school authorities learn that certain students are sexting, those students can face serious consequences. An example of this is the

Cynthia Logan, the mother of Jessica Logan, testifies before an Ohio House Committee in 2011 about the cruel and potentially lethal consequences of cyberbullying. In response, lawmakers expanded the state's antibullying legislation to include cyberbullying.

case of an eighth-grade girl in Wheaton, Illinois, who in early 2014 started exchanging sexually provocative messages with a male classmate. He encouraged her to send him nude photos of herself; she refused until he sent her a photo of his genitals via Snapchat. At that point she sexted him a topless photo of

Long-Term Embarrassment

The case of antibullying advocate Allyson Pereira is an example of just how long the social and emotional repercussions of sexting a nude photo can last. When she was a sophomore at a New Jersey high school, her boyfriend broke up with her. Two months later he told her that they could get back together if she would sext him a nude photo of herself. She did as he asked. He then shared it with friends and online, and Pereira experienced serious harassment at school and on the Internet; her house was vandalized as well. With time, however, it appeared as though her troubles were coming to an end. But then, she reports: "Two years after the picture was taken, when I was eighteen and a senior in high school, I was working as a waitress when my boss told me he had heard about the picture. He told me he was going to have it sent to him, rate it, and he'd let me know what he thought. I volunteered for a local school committee and was eating lunch when a group of girls took out their phones and showed the picture to security guards. I hid in a corner while they all pointed and laughed." She said that these experiences and others changed her future plans, explaining: "I didn't go away to college because I feared my dorm mates would find out about it and hate me."

Quoted in Andrea Weckerle, "Antibullying Advocate and Sexting Victim Allyson Pereira Shares Her Story," CiviliNation, October 25, 2011. www.civilination.org.

herself in the shower, intending for it to remain private. Instead, the boy forwarded this photo to friends, and at least one of them posted it online. When school authorities learned about this, they suspended the girl and banned her from attending her graduation ceremony because she had initiated the behavior.

Other cases result in suspensions targeting not just those who initiated the sexting but all those who participated in it. For example, in March 2014 at least a dozen young teens in Desloge, Missouri, were suspended after five or six middle-school girls sexted nude cell phone photos of themselves to boys at their school. Of their punishment, North St. Francois County School District Superintendent Yancy Poorman says,

"It's unfortunate and I'm terribly concerned, but ultimately it might be the most important lesson learned this year . . . one involving morals, values, self-respect and consequences for the 530 seventh and eighth graders at North County Middle [School]."[60]

Blackmail

Teens who want to avoid such consequences can be easy targets for blackmailers. The media sometimes calls blackmailing incidents associated with sexting *sextortion*. In the typical scenario a girl sexts a nude or seminude photo of herself, and the recipient then threatens to make the photo public and/or send it to family members unless the girl gives him more photos of herself. In one 2009 Wisconsin case, however, a boy pretending to be a girl sent messages online asking boys to send "her" nude photos of themselves. After the boys complied, the boy who received the photos used them to blackmail his victims into having sex with him.

In other cases the blackmailer has demanded that the victim supply him with nude or seminude photos of others. For example, a girl who had sexted a boy a nude photo of herself was told by the recipient that unless she sent him similar photos of five other girls he would send her photo to her classmates. Consequently, she used her cell phone to take photos of undressed girls in the school locker room without their knowledge and then send them to the boy.

Other times the demand involves sexual acts. This is what occurred at a Brentwood, California, middle school in 2014 as part of a sexting ring involving more than a dozen boys at several middle schools in the area. The girls who contributed photos to the sexting ring had supplied nude and seminude photos of themselves willingly, using their cell phones to both take and send the photos. However, they had done so believing the recipients would not disseminate the photos to others. But some of the boys did distribute the photos, and while authorities were investigating this situation they discovered that a fourteen-year-old boy had used a threat of distribution to force a girl to engage in sexual acts with him. As a result, the boy was charged with a felony.

Legal Charges

In another case, seventeen-year-old Jesse Colton Grimes of Boone, North Carolina, was charged in November 2014 with felonious first-degree sexual exploitation of a minor, felonious second-degree sexual exploitation of a minor, and felonious third-degree sexual exploitation of a minor and felonious extortion after coercing at least ten young people into sexting him nude photos. (The charge of exploitation means the images were transmitted by phone or computer; the charge of extortion is the associated blackmail.) His victims were from three states, and some of them were as young as twelve. Law enforcement authorities believe there might be at least thirty more victims of Grimes's activities and have declared him a sexual predator. Lieutenant Chris Hatton, Boone Police Department of Criminal Investigations commander, refused to provide details of this case. However, he explained that predators in general will not only blackmail their victims into sending more nude photos but often will try to set up an in-person meeting.

Teenagers who are not predators can also face serious charges for sexting. In several cases teens have faced child pornography charges for sexting sexually explicit photos of one another even though the participants were all friends, and their sexts were shared willingly. Even if those charged do not end up in jail, they can suffer from having to deal with the trauma and expense of being caught up in the criminal justice system.

Phone Evidence

There have also been cases of teens getting into legal trouble not because they shared a sexted sexually explicit photo with others but because they simply had one on their cell phone. One particularly notable case began in 2009, when the cell phone of a seventeen-year-old Pennsylvania girl, "NN," was confiscated by one of her teachers and turned over to the principal. (The girl had been talking on her phone before homeroom, despite the fact that her school banned the use of cell phones on school grounds.) The principal looked through the phone's photos, found seminude and nude photos that the girl had taken of herself, and contacted law enforcement authorities. NN reports: "He told me that he found explicit photos on my phone and that he sent it away to a crime lab. I was really embarrassed, humiliated, because it was personal."[61]

Until then the photos had not been viewed by anyone else, and they were intended for no one but the girl's boyfriend. Nonetheless, NN was suspended for three days and charged with possessing child pornography. However, the cell phone had been searched illegally, so the American Civil Liberties Union (ACLU), which protects people's rights, stepped forward to defend NN. Consequently, the charges were dropped, and NN and her attorneys received $33,000 as a settlement in a lawsuit against the school district.

But some teens are not lucky enough to have their charges dropped. In April 2014 three Arkansas teens—aged twelve, thirteen, and fourteen—were arrested for exchanging sexually explicit videos using their phones. They faced a period of probation or possibly time in juvenile detention. In a 2013 teen sexting case in Virginia, one boy spent three days in a juvenile detention facility for using his smartphone to film two consensual sex acts, which he then sexted. During his sentencing the judge said, "Your deliberate actions over a period of time made something that should have been personal and private into something cheap and nasty."[62]

Permanence

Not only can sexted images become something cheap and nasty, but they can also be permanent. A sexually provocative or explicit photo or video that has been posted online might be called forth by a search engine years later. This means that problems that occurred when the photo was first posted, such as embarrassment and harassment, can recur whenever the photo is rediscovered via online searches. It also means that prospective employers, college admissions officers, and others searching the Internet for information on a particular person will likely find that person's sex-charged photos.

Surveys have shown that people in a position to offer jobs or admission to college are increasingly likely to search the Internet for information on applicants. In fact, according to one study, the number of college admissions officers who looked at applicants' Facebook pages rose from 10 percent in 2008 to more than 30 percent in 2013. In another survey more than one-fourth of college admissions officers reported that they had Googled applicants' names, and 35 percent reported that they had seen something online that was negative enough to lessen the applicant's chances of being admitted into college. A 2013 *Forbes* magazine survey of employers found that 65 percent consider digital footprints—the impression that a per-

A college admissions officer reviews student applications. A teen's chances of being admitted to college could be harmed if sexted images or messages surface during the application process.

son's online activities makes—as part of the decision to hire someone.

The increasing importance of one's digital reputation means that just one instance of sexting-gone-viral can do a lifetime of damage. Moreover, because of the vast reach of the Internet, a person's reputation can be a global one. As the community service minister of Australia's state government of New South Wales, Linda Burney, says: "It is frightening to think that once these images are online or on a phone, anyone anywhere in the world can access them. It is then impossible to retrieve and delete them. They are there forever and can damage future career prospects or relationships."[63] Yet many teens do not think of such consequences before they take a sexy photo on their phones and hit send.

Chapter Four

Addressing
the Issue

Experts have found that it is hard to convince teens not to engage in sexting. In part this is because social media indirectly encourage such behavior. Steve Mintz, a University of Texas at Austin history professor who has written about how adolescent behavior in America has changed over time, explains: "Proponents of social media celebrate the idea that the private should be public, that intimacy is not to be secreted away. And this rejection of reticence is embraced by many young people."[64]

Mintz adds that rebellion is part of adolescence, and anything considered to be old-fashioned is to be rebelled against. He reports: "Transgression is a key theme in contemporary youth culture. This kind of exhibitionism is viewed as a pointed rejection of outmoded taboos about the body and sexuality."[65]

Other experts note that teens are also unlikely to avoid sexting because they do not believe they will get in trouble for it. Indeed, the number of teens who get into trouble because of sexting is relatively small in relation to the number of teens who sext. According to Amy Adele Hasinoff, the author of *Sexting Panic: Rethinking Criminalization, Privacy, and Consent*, further research is necessary to determine just how often private sexts are distributed without permission. However, she notes that experts generally believe this occurs roughly 10 percent of the time.

But this means that as many as one in ten sexting teens might be experiencing such a violation of privacy, and parents and school administrators believe this is too many. Consequently, they have tried to convince young people that sending one another sexually explicit messages and images is a dangerous behavior. Tech companies have tried to support adults in this effort by creating apps that make the activity more difficult, while lawmakers have attempted to make it more painful for teens to sext by passing laws that punish young people for engaging in the activity. But there is disagreement regarding whether these attempts to address the issue of teen sexting are effective or even necessary.

Parental Efforts

Although experts say that educating teens about sexting should begin at home, many also say that most parents do not understand what sexting is or what its consequences might be. This lack of authority on the subject can make it difficult if not impossible for them to convince teens that sexting is a bad idea. And even when parents do know about the possible consequences of sexting, they can have problems communicating this information to teens because their tendency is to focus on the direst consequences that can come from sexting and exaggerate the associated risks. For example, they might make it sound as though the majority of teens have their nude selfies shared without their permission, despite evidence to the contrary.

Such exaggerations can cause teens to distrust all other information parents provide. Elizabeth Englander explains:

> Why should you trust a warning that contains inaccurate data? Imagine that I warned you to wear your seat belt, because half of the car rides in America end up with someone going through the windshield. You might not listen to me, given that it's obvious to anyone that half of the car rides in America don't end up with people slamming on the brakes, much less going through the windshield. Sexting warnings are the same. If our information isn't correct, if we're issuing dire warnings about outcomes that are, in reality, pretty rare, then our message isn't heard.[66]

Implementing Controls

Another approach that parents take in trying to address the problem of sexting is to monitor their children's cell phone use. This sometimes proves effective. Studies have shown that roughly one-third of teenagers who do not sext have shied away from the activity because their parents monitor and/or limit their cell phone use. This makes sense, because as District Attorney Steve Howe of Johnson County, Missouri, says, "Kids aren't stupid, and if you tell them, 'I'm gonna check' and even if you just check a couple times, guess what? That is enough for them to say, 'Well I need to be careful about what I use this phone for because I know my parents would follow up on that.'"[67]

> "If our information isn't correct, if we're issuing dire warnings about outcomes that are, in reality, pretty rare, then our message isn't heard."[66]
>
> —Professor of psychology Elizabeth Englander.

To aid parents in controlling their teens' sexting behavior, some companies offer antisexting software that can allow parents to view their teens' text messages and the websites they have visited. In addition, some antisexting software will block a phone's access to specific websites and/or limit the times of day that the phone can be used. There is also software in development that will enable parents to be warned if a teen is sending inappropriate messages or images. For example, a type of software patented by Apple would determine whether a message had certain unauthorized words, delete the words from the message before allowing it to be sent, and then notify parents of the event.

Another type of antisexting software being developed would involve image recognition. This would allow photos to be classified based on attributes such as colors, shades, and textures. Consequently if an image that a teen is viewing, sending, or posting appears to be showing too much skin, a parent would be alerted.

Some parents monitor their teen's cell phone and social media habits. They hope that fear of being caught will prevent these young people from sexting.

But while such controls can be successful, they do not prevent a teen from borrowing a friend's unmonitored, unblocked phone in order to take a photo and sext it. As Raychelle Cassada Lohmann reports: "It's not uncommon for friends of the 'restricted' teen to let him or her borrow their phone or come to their house to use their equipment. In addition, some teens are quite clever and can still manage to get online at home all while covering their digital tracks."[68]

Educational Programs

Therefore some experts say that merely installing blocking software or taking away a teen's phone is not the way to curtail teen sexting. Instead, they argue, teens need to develop an aversion to sexting that will keep them from engaging in the activity even when no one is monitoring their behavior, and professional antisexting education programs can help them do this. Such programs make teens aware of the possible consequences of sexting without exaggerating the risks, while also typically providing opportunities for teens to discuss sexting-related issues with peers.

Photographic Proof

A sexting case in 2014 involving a seventeen-year-old boy from Manassas, Virginia, caused a great deal of outrage when people learned police intended to photograph his genitals in an aroused state. The boy had sexted nude photos of his genitals to his fifteen-year-old girlfriend. When the sexted photos came to light he was charged with felonies for manufacturing and possessing child pornography. Prosecutors wanted to match the sexted pictures to the police photos to prove the boy's guilt. But people found it offensive that law enforcement authorities were going to force the boy to become aroused. As *Salon* magazine columnist Jenny Kutner says, "Law enforcement officials . . . have come up with a truly creative way to combat the dissemination of child pornography: create more child pornography for comparison!" Others questioned why the boy was being treated so harshly while the girl was being treated like a victim; she faced no charges even though she apparently was the one who started sexting sexually explicit images with him in the first place. Given the reaction to their approach to the case, the police announced that they would not be taking the pictures after all and would allow the court order authorizing the photographs to expire.

Quoted in Anthony Zurcher, "Teen Sexting Prosecution Prompts Outrage," BBC News, July 10, 2014. www.bbc.com.

This approach appears to be successful at least when it comes to getting teens to understand the possible legal consequences of sexting. According to a 2014 study at Drexel University in Philadelphia, Pennsylvania, educational programs that make teens aware that it is a crime to sext nude photos of minors deter some teens from sexting. Therefore experts recommend that more funding be spent on establishing such educational programs at schools.

Some schools already offer such programs as part of their curriculum. For example, through a statewide initiative, Idaho addresses sexting via Digital Technology & Teen Relationships presentations at high schools. Provided by the Center for Healthy Relationships, which is associated with a nonprofit organization called the Idaho Coalition Against Sexual & Domestic Violence, these presentations use group activities to engage teens in discussions about the consequences of sexting.

Many other nonprofit organizations also work with schools to help educate teens about sexting. One of the most notable is the Common Sense Media, which provides information, classroom tools, and lesson materials to teachers on various digital issues, including sexting. In their lesson materials on sexting, they explain why it is a bad idea to sext, and they talk about such issues as how to deal with peer pressure and what to do upon receiving an unsolicited sext.

Another group that seeks to educate teens is Break the Cycle. Through its Love Is Not Abuse program, it provides educational material on digital abuse and how it factors into dating violence. The group considers sexting a form of digital abuse, which it says can involve hurtful activities done by someone who did not necessarily intend to cause harm. This same sentiment is shared in MTV's online campaign called A Thin Line, which was established to help teens recognize and combat all forms of digital abuse. The name of the campaign comes from the fact that there is a thin line between something harmless and something harmful.

Nonprofit organizations also provide educational programs for use outside of school. For example, the National Center for

Missing and Exploited Children (NCMEC) addresses sexting as part of its online interactive program NetSmartz Workshop. The program provides online safety education for young people, parents, educators, and law enforcement.

Other organizations focus on aiding those who have been harmed by sexting. One such organization is Without My Consent, which provides resources for teens who have been abused via sexting and/or online harassment. It also supports efforts to create laws to fight online harassment, reputational harm, and other issues related to digital abuse. In addition, it has conducted surveys related to online stalking, harassment, and violations of privacy.

A Criminal Justice Problem

In some states the criminal justice system also incorporates educational programs into its response to teen sexting. For example, Texas mandates that minors who have been convicted of a sexting-related crime take an online course called the Sexting Prevention Educational Program. Similarly, New York enacted a sexting-specific law in 2012 that allows teens who have been caught sexting to avoid being subjected to tough criminal penalties by attending educational programs. Prior to enacting this law, teens who engaged in consensual sexting might have been sentenced to time in jail under child pornography laws. These laws made no provisions for teaching them about the risks inherent in sexting and how they might avoid peer pressure to sext.

Today many states still rely solely on child pornography laws to address teen sexting crimes, believing that harsh punishments are the best way to deter young people from engaging in the activity. However, this approach began to be criticized in 2009 thanks to extensive media coverage of a case of teen sexting in Greensburg, Pennsylvania. Specifically, after three teenage girls in Greensburg sent nude selfies to three male classmates the girls were charged with manufacturing and distributing child pornography, and the boys were charged with possessing child pornography. Many people were outraged at the idea that a consensual and seemingly harmless act might result in six teenagers going to prison.

As a result of the interest in this case, the media called attention to other cases in which teens had been treated harshly for sexting. One of these cases was that of eighteen-year-old Phillip Alpert of Florida. Alpert was convicted in 2009 of distributing child pornography because he had sent sexually explicit selfies of his girlfriend to dozens of friends and family members after the couple had a fight. He was sentenced to five years probation and required to be listed as a registered sex offender for the next twenty-five years. (Registered sex offenders are not allowed to live in places or hold jobs that would put them in proximity to minors).

About his sentence, Alpert complains, "You will find me on the registered sex offender list next to people who have raped

Phillip Alpert was kicked out of college and could not find a job after he was forced to register as a sex offender. Alpert earned the criminal record for e-mailing nude photos of his teenage girlfriend to friends after the couple had a fight.

children, molested kids, things like that, because I sent child pornography. You think child pornography, you think 6-year-old, 3-year-old little kids who can't think for themselves, who are taken advantage of. That really wasn't the case." Instead, he says, he simply did "a stupid thing . . . because I was upset and tired and it was the middle of the night and I was an immature kid."[69]

Legal Penalties

National attention to cases such as this, along with the resulting public pressure, has inspired state legislatures to act. Some have passed laws that made sexting a crime separate from child pornography. As of September 2014 twenty states have sexting laws; some focus on the activities of minors while others also address sexting by people over eighteen. Sexting laws also vary from state to state in regard to what acts constitute a sexting crime and how such crimes are punished if a person is convicted of them.

Many experts consider these variances a serious problem. David DeMatteo explains why:

Laws work best when they are clear, consistent and predictable, so having different legal definitions of sexting in different jurisdictions can be confusing. Moreover, sexting behavior that is legal in one state may lead to criminal charges in a neighboring state. An interesting question is what happens if someone sends a sext that is legal in their jurisdiction to a person in a jurisdiction in which that sext could be the basis of criminal charges. Which law governs in that situation—the law of the state in which the sext was sent or the law of state in which the sext was received.[70]

Some of the laws, in addition to differing from state to state, are far from straightforward. In Texas, for instance, it is a crime for anyone under the age of seventeen to send or keep a sexually explicit image. However, Texas does not consider this to be a crime if both are minors who are dating each other and are no more than two years apart in age. This approach was adopted in order to recognize the fact that two teens close in age who are involved in a dating relationship are likely sexting one another willingly as part of an intimate relationship rather than as one teen's attempt to take advantage of the other. In contrast, Arizona's approach is to ignore the relationship between the teens and focus on keeping those who unwillingly receive a sext from being punished for it. Consequently, in this state it is a crime for a minor of any age to receive a sexually explicit photo except when the minor did not request the photo and either deleted it or reported it to an authority figure.

> "Sexting behavior that is legal in one state may lead to criminal charges in a neighboring state."[70]
>
> —David DeMatteo, a professor of law and psychology at Drexel University.

Punishments

In terms of punishments, some states treat sexting crimes as misdemeanors and some as felonies, based on lawmakers' beliefs regarding whether harsh punishments for sexting can serve as a deterrent. The lightest punishments (misdemeanors) reflect the belief that teens who sext illegally have simply made a stupid mistake and need to understand why they should never do it again. In Pennsylvania, for example, the sexting law encourages judges to order the offender to complete an educational program rather than to sentence him or her to jail. If the program is successfully completed, then the conviction is wiped from the minor's criminal record, and it will be as though the sexting never occurred.

But in other states lawmakers believe that it is not necessarily enough just to sentence a convicted teen sexter to attend an

Revenge Porn

California has no sexting law, but in October 2013 it adopted the first law to address cases where someone disseminates a nude photo as an act of revenge. The first person convicted under the revenge porn law was thirty-six-year-old Noe Iniguez of Los Angeles. In December 2014 he posted nude photos of his ex-girlfriend without her consent on her employer's Facebook page, accompanied by derogatory comments and suggestions that she be fired. As a result he was sentenced to a year in jail and thirty-six months of probation, and he will have to attend counseling. He was also ordered to have no contact with his victim. As of December 2014 ten other states had passed revenge porn laws.

educational program. Instead, depending on the circumstances surrounding the sexting, certain teens should be made to atone for their actions by performing community service or paying a fine. For example, in Florida a first-time teen offender who has been found guilty of sending or receiving a nude image deemed harmful to a minor might be ordered to perform eight hours of community service or pay a sixty-dollar fine and/or participate in a class on sexting. A second offense in Florida is considered a misdemeanor, but a third offense is a felony and therefore might involve jail time.

Other states, such as Georgia, give prosecutors the ability to charge a sexting crime as either a misdemeanor or a felony. The decision may depend on whether the offender has harassed, intimidated, embarrassed, or otherwise hurt anyone. In deciding how to charge a case, prosecutors might also take into account whether the defendant is remorseful and therefore unlikely to offend again. This is in keeping with the spirit in which many lawmakers enacted teen sexting laws. Their aim was not to jail teens caught sexting but to make sure that such teens would never want to sext again.

The Threat of a Felony

This approach is favored by the majority of the American public. According to a University of Michigan survey released in 2012, 81 percent of Americans believe that education programs and counseling are the appropriate punishment for teen sexters. Seventy-five percent also support community service as a punishment. In contrast, only 20 percent believe sexting teens should be prosecuted under child pornography laws.

States without sexting laws, however, have no other recourse than to charge people who send and/or receive sexually explicit photos with felonies under child pornography laws. (Making, possessing, and/or distributing child pornography is always a felony.) Nonetheless, prosecutors have some discretion on how to proceed with a sexting-related case. First, it is up to them to determine whether the sexted photo is pornographic, since it is not always obvious whether the subject of such a photo is in a state of sexual excitement or posed in a sexually-explicit manner. If the prosecutor decides that the image is not pornography, then the charges are dropped. Second, the prosecutor can decide to negotiate a sentencing deal with the defendant rather than taking the case to trial. This means the sexter will get a more lenient sentence than the court would have awarded. Attorney Ray Morrogh of Virginia, which has no sexting law and therefore prosecutes sexters under its child pornography law, explains, "We try to resolve these cases wherever possible without going to the courts. At the juvenile level, the goal is to rehabilitate the child."[71]

Arguments over Leniency

Experts have noted that prosecutors in states without sexting laws are increasingly taking this approach in cases where teens have been arrested for harmless sexting. In Maryland, which has no sexting law, state attorney Anne Colt Leitess reports that cases of teens posting sexually explicit photos online are on the rise—and even becoming commonplace. Even so, she adds, it has become rare for a sexting case to make it to court.

This pleases people who believe that harmless sexting should not be treated as a crime. This is the view of Marsha Levick of the Juvenile Law Center. She says, "Why should we criminalize a kid for taking and possessing a photo of herself?"[72]

Other experts point out that if teens do become afraid of being arrested for sexting, they will become even more secretive about their sexting activities. As Elizabeth Schroeder, executive director of the national sexuality education organization Answer, notes, a policy of punishing teens for sexting "teaches them that it's unsafe to talk with an adult about sexting because they risk being charged with a crime. It is ridiculously short-sighted."[73]

But others counter that even if teens are not jailed for sexting, the punishment should be severe so it can serve as an example to others. To this end some have suggested that teens be subjected to hefty fines. For example, blogger Paul Metheney says in regard to a case of teens forwarding a sexually explicit selfie video, "EVERY kid that forwarded the video [including the girl who made the selfie] should be fined so severely that it sparks a national tidal wave of parents talking to their kids about the responsibilities and privilege of using a phone, a computer or a brain."[74]

It is unclear, though, whether a hefty fine would serve as a deterrent—especially given the fact that the teen's parents would be the ones most likely paying it. But studies do suggest that fear of being jailed will not deter teens from sexting. In fact, they show that teens are more afraid of being punished by parents for sexting or being disapproved of by peers for not sexting than they are of being arrested by police because of their sexting activities.

Interviews with teens also indicate that young people do not worry about potential criminal charges when they consider

> "Why should we criminalize a kid for taking and possessing a photo of herself?"[72]
>
> —Marsha Levick, legal director of the Juvenile Law Center.

whether to sext. For example, seventeen-year-old Kat of San Francisco, California, who is thinking of getting into sexting because all her friends are doing it, reports: "I have a boyfriend now, and sometimes I feel like it might lighten the mood or make things fun. To be honest, I didn't even think about the legal stuff at all."[75]

Considering the Choices

More often young people are thinking about the positives of sharing sexts with a current or prospective boyfriend or girlfriend. For example, Lauren, a college student who engages in sexting with a long-distance boyfriend, says, "In a mature relationship with someone I trust and am able to talk to, sexting can be really nice. It reminds us of being together, even when we can't be."[76] Consequently she and others like her will probably continue to sext, and ultimately it will be up to them to make the choice as to just how sexually explicit their sexts will be and just how much they are willing to risk to share them.

Source Notes

Introduction: Unforeseen Consequences

1. Quoted in Amanda Lenhart, "Teens and Sexting," Pew Internet & American Life Project, December 2009. www.nc dsv.org.

2. Quoted in Lenhart, "Teens and Sexting."

3. Quoted in Pam Horne, "Teens Engaged in Sexting, Cyberbullying Face Potential Felony Charges," *Williamson Herald* (Franklin, TN), February 23, 2014. www.williamsonherald .com.

4. Quoted in Gigi Stone, "'Sexting' Teens Can Go Too Far," ABC News, March 13, 2009. abcnews.go.com.

5. Quoted in Drexel University, "Majority of Minors Engage in Sexting, Unaware of Legal Consequences," news release, *Social Work Today*. www.socialworktoday.com.

6. Quoted in Hanna Rosin, "Why Kids Sext," *Atlantic*, October 14, 2014. www.theatlantic.com.

Chapter One: What Is the Point of Sexting?

7. Quoted in Alex McKechnie, "Sexting Among Minors: A Q+A About New Study," *Drexel News Blog*, June 18, 2014. http://newsblog.drexel.edu.

8. Quoted in *New York Times*, "What They're Saying About Sexting," March 26, 2011. www.nytimes.com.

9. Quoted in *New York Times*, "What They're Saying About Sexting."

10. Quoted in BBC News, "Sexting Survey Shows Pressure Faced by Teens," October 16, 2013. www.bbc.com.

11. Quoted in KCCI 8 News, "Six Teens Charged in Sexting Case," November 21, 2012. www.kcci.com.

12. Quoted in ABC 7, "West Springfield High School Teen Sexting Case in Court," April 18, 2013. www.wjla.com.

13. Quoted in Vincenza Previte, "Sexting: What Parents and Teenagers Should Know," Stop Sexting. www.stop-sexting .com.

14. Quoted in Rosin, "Why Kids Sext."

15. James Hamblin, "It's Not Just About Showing Your Genitals: Time to Talk About Sexting," *Atlantic*, September 18, 2012. www.theatlantic.com.

16. Quoted in *New York Times*, "What They're Saying About Sexting."

17. Andy Phippen, "Sexting: An Exploration of Practices, Attitudes, and Influences," UK Safer Internet Center, December 2012. www.nspcc.org.uk.

18. Quoted in Claudia Feldman, "When Texting Turns to Sexting, the Trouble Begins," Chron, April 5, 2009. www.chron. com.

19. Quoted in Amanda Hess, "The Real Difference Between Teenage Boys and Girls' Sexting Habits? Boys Forward More," *Slate*, March 4, 2013. www.slate.com.

20. Quoted in Jessica Chasmar, "Teen Sexting Is the New 'First Base,' Study Shows," *Washington Times*, October 6, 2014. www.washingtontimes.com.

21. Quoted in Rick Nauert, "Is Sexting Normal?," Psych Central, October 7, 2014. http://psychcentral.com.

22. Sameer Hinduja, "What Jennifer Lawrence Can Teach Us About Sexting Among Teens," Cyberbullying Research Center, October 8, 2014. http://cyberbullying.us.

23. Quoted in Sue Shellenbarger, "Why Do Teens Engage in 'Sexting?,'" *The Juggle* (blog), June 15, 2009. http://blogs .wsj.com.

24. Quoted in Rosin, "Why Kids Sext."

25. Quoted in Rosin, "Why Kids Sext."

26. Quoted in Lenhart, "Teens and Sexting."

27. Quoted in Lori Higgins, "Teens Might Face Felony Charges for Texting," *USA Today*, October 16, 2014. www.usatoday .com.

28. Quoted in *New York Times,* "What They're Saying About Sexting."

29. Quoted in Lenhart, "Teens and Sexting."

30. BBC News, "Sexting Survey Shows Pressure Faced by Teens."

31. Quoted in McKechnie, "Sexting Among Minors."

Chapter Two: Outside Influences

32. Quoted in Jason DeRusha, "Teen Shares Sexting Story, Tells Parents 'Don't Be Naïve,'" CBS Minnesota, November 12, 2014. http://minnesota.cbslocal.com.

33. Quoted in DeRusha, "Teen Shares Sexting Story."

34. Quoted in DeRusha, "Teen Shares Sexting Story."

35. Quoted in Christina Caron, "Teen Sexting Linked to Psychological Distress," *Good Morning America*, ABC News, November 10, 2011. abcnews.go.com.

36. Quoted in Abigail Pesta, "Boys Also Harmed by Teen 'Hook-Up' Culture, Experts Say," NBC News, August 14, 2013. www.nbcnews.com.

37. Quoted in Anne Collier, "Sexting: Parents Need to Understand Social Pressures and Behavior," *Christian Science Monitor*, July 11, 2012. www.csmonitor.com.

38. Nancy Jo Sales, "Friends Without Benefits," *Vanity Fair*, September 26, 2013. www.vanityfair.com.

39. Abigail M. Judge, "'Sexting' Among US Adolescents: Psychological and Legal Perspectives," *Harvard Review of Psychiatry*, vol. 20, 2012, pp. 86–96. http://abigailjudge.com.

40. Quoted in Sales, "Friends Without Benefits."

41. Quoted in Susan Smith, "How Sexting Culture Sets Women Up to Fail," *Daily Dot*, as reposted on *The Week*, June 28, 2014. http://theweek.com.

42. Quoted in Sales, "Friends Without Benefits."

43. Jack, "Jack Says Sexting Is Part of Today's Culture," *Daily Collegian*, Penn State University, March 20, 2014. www.collegian.psu.edu.

44. *Daily Telegraph* (Sydney, AU), "Snapchat Sexting and the Predators of Kik: The Apps Your Children Need to Stay Away From," June 7, 2014. www.dailytelegraph.com.au.

45. Judge, "'Sexting' Among US Adolescents."

46. Judge, "'Sexting' Among US Adolescents."

47. Quoted in Judge, "'Sexting' Among US Adolescents."

48. Scarlett Brown, "Young People, Technology, and the 'Problem' of Sexting," in "Sociology Lens," Society Pages, April 20, 2013. http://thesocietypages.org.

Chapter Three: The Consequences of Sexting

49. Elizabeth Englander, "Stop Demonizing Teen Sexting. In Most Cases It's Completely Harmless," *Washington Post*, November 7, 2014. www.washingtonpost.com.

50. Quoted in CBC News, "Montreal Teen Says She Regrets Sexting with Classmates," November 21, 2013. www.cbc.ca.

51. Quoted in Jan Hoffman, "A Girl's Nude Photo, and Altered Lives," *New York Times*, March 27, 2011. www.nytimes.com.

52. Quoted in Hoffman, "A Girl's Nude Photo, and Altered Lives."

53. Quoted in Hoffman, "A Girl's Nude Photo, and Altered Lives."

54. Quoted in Hoffman, "A Girl's Nude Photo, and Altered Lives."

55. Quoted in Hoffman, "A Girl's Nude Photo, and Altered Lives."

56. Raychelle Cassada Lohmann, "The Dangers of Teen Sexting," *Psychology Today*, July 20, 2012. www.psychology today.com.

57. Quoted in Caron, "Teen Sexting Linked to Psychological Distress."

58. ChildLine, "James—My Experience of Sexting." www.child line.org.uk.

59. Cynthia Logan, posting as CYNSJRL, February 15, 2014, comments section of CBS News, "Mom's Fight to End Cyberabuse," May 14, 2009. www.cbsnews.com.

60. Quoted in Leisa Zigman, "Desloge Middle School Students Suspended for Sexting," KSDK, March 28, 2014. www.ks dk.com.

61. Quoted in CBS News, "'Sexting' Leads to Child Porn Charges for Teens," June 5, 2010. www.cbsnews.com.

62. Quoted in John Henrehan, "Short Jail Sentence for Fairfax County Teen Involved in 'Sexting,'" Fox 5 WTTG, June 12, 2013. www.myfoxdc.com.

63. Quoted in Belinda Goldsmith, "Safe 'Sexting'? No Such Thing, Teens Warned," Reuters, May 4, 2009. www.reuters .com.

Chapter Four: Addressing the Issue

64. Quoted in Gracie Bonds Staples, "How Much Should You Worry About Teens' Sexting?," *Atlanta Journal Constitution*, December 19, 2013. www.myajc.com.

65. Quoted in Staples, "How Much Should You Worry About Teens' Sexting?"

66. Elizabeth Englander, "Everything You Wanted to Know About Sexting but Were Afraid to Ask," The Conversation, November 6, 2014. http://theconversation.com.

67. Quoted in Jeanene Kiesling, "Prosecutors Warn Teens About Perils of Sexting," KCTV5, February 25, 2013. www.kctv5.com.

68. Raychelle Cassada Lohmann, "Teens Who Click, Send, and Text," in *Teen Angst*, blog, *Psychology Today*, August 7, 2013. www.psychologytoday.com.

69. Quoted in Deborah Feyerick and Sheila Steffen, "'Sexting' Lands Teen on Sex Offender List," CNN, April 7, 2009. www.cnn.com.

70. Quoted in McKechnie, "Sexting Among Minors."

71. Quoted in Justin Jouvenal, "Teen 'Sexting' Case Fuels Debate over Punishment," *Washington Post*, April 18, 2013. www.azcentral.com.

72. Quoted in CBS News, "'Sexting' Leads to Child Porn Charges for Teens."

73. Quoted in Martha Kempner, "Punish First, Educate Later: South Carolina Lawmakers' Approach to Teen Sexting Is Backwards at Best," RH Reality Check, January 25, 2012. http://rhrealitycheck.org.

74. Paul Metheney, "About This Blog," *From the Hip*. http://paulmetheney.com.

75. Quoted in Alyssa Giacobbe, "Can Sexting Get You Arrested?," *Teen Vogue*. www.teenvogue.com.

76. Quoted in Giacobbe, "Can Sexting Get You Arrested?"

Break the Cycle

6029 Bristol Pkwy., Suite 201
Culver City, CA 90230
phone: (310) 286-3383
website: breakthecycle.org

A national nonprofit organization, Break the Cycle works to educate and empower young people to free themselves from domestic violence. To this end the group engages in educational efforts related to domestic and dating violence and abuse.

Common Sense Media

650 Townsend, Suite 435
San Francisco, CA 94103
phone: (415) 863-0600
website: commonsensemedia.org

Common Sense Media provides information and advice related to media and technology. The organization's aim is to help people make smart choices when they go online. It also works with teachers and others to create educational programs related to digital safety issues, including sexting.

ConnectSafely

website: ConnectSafely.org

This is a nonprofit organization that provides information to teens, parents, educators, and others on issues related to online social networks, digital media, and technology. ConnectSafely provides discussion forums, articles, videos, safety tips, and other material related to staying safe online.

iKeepSafe (Internet Keep Safe Coalition)

4301 N. Fairfax Dr., Suite 190
Arlington, VA 22203
phone: (703) 717-9066
fax: (703) 852-7100 ATTN: iKeepSafe
e-mail: info@ikeepsafe.org

iKeepSafe is a nonprofit international alliance of policy leaders, educators, law enforcement members, technology experts, public health experts, and others committed to helping young people stay safe online. To this end it provides educators, parents, and young people with information on high-risk digital activities such as sexting.

NetSmartz Workshop

Charles B. Wang International
Children's Building
699 Prince St.
Alexandria, VA 22314-3175
phone: (800) 843-5678

An interactive, educational program of the National Center for Missing & Exploited Children (NCMEC), NetSmartz Workshop provides information to children aged five to seventeen, parents, educators, and law enforcement officials to help ensure that young people understand the risks of certain Internet activities.

A Thin Line

website: www.athinline.org

A campaign established by MTV, A Thin Line aims to empower young people to identify, respond to, and stop the spread of digital abuse in their lives and the lives of their peers. The campaign's name refers to the thin line between harmless activities and ones that lead to serious consequences, such as sexting.

Wired Safety

website: www.wiredsafety.org

A grassroots group staffed entirely by volunteers, Wired Safety provides information on issues related to Internet safety, security, privacy, and responsibility and works to educate people about online dangers. The group also helps victims of harassment and crimes related to online activities.

Without My Consent

website: withoutmyconsent.org

Founded by experts in Internet and privacy issues, Without My Consent is a nonprofit organization dedicated to combating online invasions of privacy. The information provided by its website is intended to empower individuals to stand up for their privacy rights and to educate them on issues such as free speech and online invasions of privacy.

For Further Research

Books

Danah Boyd, *It's Complicated: The Social Lives of Networked Teens*. New Haven, CT: Yale University Press, 2014.

Judith Davidson, *Sexting: Gender and Teens.* Boston: Sense, 2014.

Amy Adele Hasinoff, *Sexting Panic: Rethinking Criminalization, Privacy, and Consent*. Champaign, IL: University of Illinois Press, 2015.

Sameer K. Hinduja and Justin W. Patchin, *Bullying Beyond the Schoolyard: Preventing and Responding to Cyberbullying.* Thousand Oaks, CA: Corwin, 2014.

Rebecca T. Klein, *Frequently Asked Questions About Texting, Sexting, and Flaming* (FAQ: Teen Life series). New York: Rosen, 2013.

Carol Langlois, *Girl Talk: Boys, Bullies, and Body Image*. Madison, VA: Christine F. Anderson, 2014.

Shaheen Shariff, *Sexting and Cyberbullying: Defining the Line for Digitally Empowered Kids.* New York: Cambridge University Press, 2015.

Internet Sources

Andrew J. Harris, Judith Davidson, Elizabeth Letourneau, Carl Paternite, and Karin Tusinski Miofsky, "Building a Prevention Framework to Address Teen 'Sexting' Behaviors," US Department of Justice. www.ncjrs.gov/pdffiles1/ojjdp/grants/244001.pdf.

Abigail M. Judge, "'Sexting' Among US Adolescents: Psychological and Legal Perspectives," *Harvard Review of Psychiatry*, vol. 20, 2012, pp. 86–96. http://abigailjudge.com/img/amj-hrp -2012.pdf.

Janine Zweig and Meredith Dank, "Teen Dating Abuse and Harassment in the Digital World: Implications for Prevention and Treatment," February 2013. www.urban.org/Uploaded PDF/412750-teen-dating-abuse.pdf.

Index

Picture Credits

Patricia D. Netzley is the author of dozens of books for children, teens, and adults. She writes both fiction and nonfiction and is a member of the Society of Children's Book Writers and Illustrators.